COURAGE

does not always Roar

Ordinary Women with Extraordinary Courage

BOBI SEREDICH

FOREWORD : *Mary Anne Radmacher*

Published by Simple Truths, an imprint of Sourcebooks
P.O. Box 4410, Naperville, Illinois 60567-4410
(630) 961-3900
sourcebooks.com

Design: Lynn Harker, Simple Truths, Illinois
Edited by: Alice Patenaude

Printed and bound in the United States of America.
POD

Dedication

To my mother and Mac for believing in me when I didn't even believe in myself. I have so much gratitude for them and my dearest girlfriends and all the women that have been open and vulnerable in sharing their amazing stories of courage while teaching me so much along the way. I also want to thank my support team who encouraged me to write this book including my brother John, Mary Anne, Joelle, Gail, Vera, Tammy, Barb, G, Kristina and Cherie. Thank you to Rick for my photograph, and Chelsea and Shae for their love. Thank you to my editor, Alice, who helped me to write the "right" message and Lynn for all of her beautiful design work. I want to give a very special thank you to Roy - my love, best friend and biggest fan. Most importantly, I thank God everyday for the gift of life!!

Table of Contents

Introduction

When we think about courage, it's usually stories of heroism that come to mind—saving someone from a fire or climbing Mount Everest. But for millions of women around the world, courage comes in a very different way. It's a quiet voice that gives them the strength to go on for another day, sometimes in the face of seemingly insurmountable odds.

This little book shares the stories of a few of those Quiet Warriors and will hopefully inspire others to face their challenges each day, renewed with the knowledge that others have survived in similar situations.

You'll read stories from a number of women who have inspired me in my own life as well as stories shared by others who have gone through turmoil to come out stronger on the other side.

I'd like to start by sharing the inspirational story behind the poem by writer Mary Anne Radmacher, a poem which has made its way around the world and is the namesake of this book.

Share your quiet voice of courage with someone else today.

Bobi Seredich

FOREWORD

By Mary Anne Radmacher

MY FRIEND CAME TO MY OFFICE IN TEARS.
Unfortunately, she also left with her tears. I listened. I listened to her frustration and feelings of uncertainty. Her adored adopted daughter came with a set of challenges for which she was in no way prepared. At the time there was little information available about intercultural adoption, but she learned what she could. She thought she was ready for the journey of being an adoptive parent.

But this? Don't we all wish we had the advantage of hindsight to offer our friends in need? Ah. If I knew then what I know now, I could have comforted her. I would have known to tell her that the challenges were not because her daughter was adopted, but rather because she was brilliant. She was bright in ways that this small community had no tools to measure and no lens to see the breadth of her capacity. How does ANY mother know how to deal with that? But I didn't know then. No one did. It seemed logical to seize the apparent. To think it all had to do with being a multi-racial family in a non-diverse community. Or to believe the challenges were tied to the adoptive transition process.

What I told her was that I admired her. I told her how I thought she was brave.

"I don't feel very brave."

"Oh, but you are. You are demonstrating the most difficult kind of courage. The kind that faces difficulty day after day. You are trying to find ways to be the sort of mother you really want to be. I just wish I could help you see what a good mother you already are."

I am not a parent myself, and I felt out of my element. But I knew I was in my element for being a good friend. So I offered what support I could. Still . . . there were tears when she left.

Her predicament stayed in my thoughts for some time. I wanted to be helpful and I thought perhaps my writing could show me something I needed to share. I wrote her a little poem I called . . .

" *Sometimes.* "

"Sometimes ... there aren't any trumpets—
   just lots of dragons.

Sometimes ... there aren't any medals to win—
   no golden chalice,
      no honor in having fought a fierce dragon.

Sometimes ... all you can say is,
   'the day is done and I tried my best.'

Sometimes the very best you can do is to keep trying."

This piece still hangs in her office.

"Sometimes" evolved into a poem which has found its way around the world—in speeches and books, eulogies and prayers, in art on walls, in blogs and on refrigerator doors. It was sketched into a *New Yorker* cartoon and featured in the Oxford Dictionary of American Quotations.

After September 11, 2001, I got a call from a client in New Jersey. She'd driven by a fire station and the "Courage" piece had been emblazoned in vinyl on a banner across a firehouse door. These were firefighters leaving their station every day to go work at ground zero in New York City's World Trade Center. It's the first thing they saw when they brought their trucks back home at the end of their arduous shifts.

When I ask people about courage, inevitably I hear stories of heroism ... of firefighters who run toward the fire, not away from it ... of daring rescues. I press further and ask about how courage looks in their own lives.

Most folks tell me they just aren't that courageous.

People are stronger than they think and more courageous than they know. In the simplest terms, courage is doing something that produces fear. What takes courage for me to do may not be what takes courage for you. We are afraid of different things—because our two actions may be different from each other doesn't mean one is more courageous than another.

My friend continued her commitment to work through her fear of not knowing what her child needed … and every day, met her child with love. In each moment, she gave of herself in the best way she knew. Each day, she tried. Her daughter has grown into a unique, talented individual who graces the world with her abilities and creativity. She is a strong and confident woman raised by a courageous mother.

The poem, as it grew in my heart became this:

courage doesn't always roar.

*sometimes courage is the quiet voice
at the end of the day saying,*

"I will try again tomorrow."

Choosing to persevere, agreeing with yourself to set down the burden of this day, and being willing to pick it up again tomorrow takes the most diligent and profound kind of courage. The strength of the "what if" casting itself as a combative question, the longing for resolution or ease in a circumstance, the fear of failure … these are all assailants that this quiet courage comes toe to toe with.

And daily, the murmured courage wins the battle.

Unlike the familiar roar in heroic tales, the courage of which I speak is often expressed in a whisper, if there's any sound at all. This courage is articulated in commitment, diligent action and an underlying belief that perhaps THIS day will be the day of victory.

And sometimes it is.
And for those times it is not ...
courage finds the way to try again ...
Tomorrow.

Here you will find stories of individuals who, like most of us, live lives that appear ordinary. And smack in the middle of it ... they are faced with a thing that causes a stack of rising, grey, smoking fear; an unexpected and unprecedented thing for which they had no preparation, training or way of knowing what to do. In the midst of an ordinary life, the people in these stories were called upon to demonstrate extraordinary courage. They each found their way. Perhaps their stories will help you find yours.

"*I think a hero is an ordinary individual who finds strength to persevere and endure in spite of overwhelming obstacles.*"

CHRISTOPHER REEVE

PERSIST

No Matter What and Overcome Your Limitations ...

My mom's entire life changed in a matter of seconds. While driving home late one night, my parents' SUV was hit from behind by a drunk driver traveling 70 miles per hour. Their car was pushed off the road and down an embankment, where it flipped several times. Dad was crushed by the impact and killed instantly. Mom was thrown from the SUV and paramedics found her on the side of the road.

My brother was in Houston when the accident happened, and I was living in Buenos Aires, Argentina, when I heard the news. We both flew home as soon we could, but I have to tell you, that was the longest flight of my entire life. I was only 28 years old at the time and never could have imagined that something so tragic would happen to my family.

Once I saw my mom in the hospital, I knew she had a long road ahead of her. She had crushing injuries to her arm and shoulder, and her elbow was dislocated in three places, leaving it permanently bent. The doctors thought they might need to amputate her arm. It was difficult for me to find a spot to touch her that was not bruised—a place to reach out and let her know, "I am here now, and somehow it will all be ok."

After a few months and nine surgeries, my mother was ready to go home and begin physical therapy on her road to recovery. Having been deeply sedated for the majority of her time in the hospital, she had just found out about my father's death and was only beginning to realize how her life had changed forever. While the hospital had helped my mother to heal, it had also taken her independence, self esteem and confidence. My mother found herself in an unfamiliar world when she entered her home. My father's energy was everywhere, but his presence was gone. How would she manage all of this? Where would she find the strength? She felt lost and helpless in her own house.

Although it took my mom a long time to physically recover from the accident, it was only a short time before my mom's positive spirit returned. She is a fiery Italian woman with the strength of character of a Buddhist monk and a heart of gold. I never doubted she would persevere and make the best of her situation. Many people would have gone into a deep depression with her circumstances. But not my mother. Her response to the situation that life handed her taught me that even though you can't control what happens to you, you can control your reaction and attitude.

Throughout her journey of recovery, my mother rarely complained. I could see the pain in her eyes during physical therapy, but never heard her question why this had happened to her. Life was tough to be sure, but Mother never lost her sense of humor. In doing so, she was able to cope more effectively and put others at ease.

In fact, I remember one "role reversal" where we both just had to laugh. Mother had lost a lot of weight during her hospital stay, so I bought her some new clothes. I had to dress her at first, but she challenged herself every day. Finally, when she was able to get dressed on her own, she looked at me in the mirror and started laughing. While she appreciated the clothes I had bought, she really hated the styles I had chosen and couldn't wait to go shopping on her own. I started laughing too; she had struggled for months to put on clothes that she didn't even like!

It reminded me of when I was in kindergarten and my mother made me wear dresses when I just wanted to wear pants. It was a funny role reversal for both of us and I understood how she felt.

Mother celebrated the small victories. At first, she had to depend on my brother or me to help her do everything. She accepted our help with grace, a smile on her face, or a little laugh about how big a production a simple task like going to the bathroom had become in her life.

It took my mom two long years to gain back her strength and limited flexibility. She still does not have full movement in her hand and will never be able to raise her arm over her head, but these limitations have not stopped her in the least. She set her mind to achieve simple goals like dressing herself and eating with her left hand, and then tackled tougher skills like cooking and driving a car.

It wasn't an easy road. It was one full of potholes and twists and turns. She had many setbacks on her journey to recovery, but she never gave up hope. *She kept a positive attitude, accepted her challenges and persevered ... trying a little harder to recover each day.* That's not to say that she didn't have sad moments and feelings of frustration, because she did, but they never lasted long. She rarely felt sorry for herself, and many times consoled other family members and friends who broke down in tears.

Those few years were a traumatic time for our entire family. Mom had to overcome many challenges. She found that strength of will and a sense of humor can get you through the toughest times, even when you don't think you have anything to smile about. My mother became a real friend to me during that time. I felt her tenderness and vulnerability, but I never forgot that she was my beautiful, strong mother—the one who showed me what real courage is all about.

"Have courage for the great sorrows of life and patience for the small ones; and when you have laboriously accomplished your daily task, go to sleep in peace. God is awake."

VICTOR HUGO

"*God grant me the serenity to accept the things I cannot change, the courage to change the things I can, and the wisdom to know the difference.*"

REINHOLD NIEBUHR

APPRECIATE
the Little Moments

Courage comes in many forms. Sometimes, it's the fortitude to keep on going day after day. One of the most courageous roles I have witnessed is that of an adult child caring for his or her parent. I experienced this role reversal first-hand for two years while caring for my mother until she regained her independence after her car accident. But, I think it is an entirely different challenge when you care for an aging parent who will never be independent again.

As the caregiver for her father, my friend, Gail, was a shining example of courage. Gail's father, Harry, was diagnosed with lower neuropathy—leaving him unable to walk steadily without aid. A second back surgery at age 80 left him in a wheelchair. Gail and her mother, Gloria, were his primary caregivers. With a rigorous daily schedule to keep Harry showered, moving, fed and inspired, it was a tremendous responsibility and there was constant fear that he would fall.

Gloria was physically and emotionally exhausted from the daily activities of taking care of her husband.

Gail was there to help her mother, but she also worked full-time. After five years, the worst happened: Gloria had a massive heart attack and died instantly. As Gail was leaving the hospital after her mother's death, they handed her a booklet on elderly care as she exited with her father in a wheelchair. It all seemed like a bad dream.

"Kind words can be short and easy to speak, but their echoes are truly endless."

MOTHER TERESA

Gail was extremely sad to lose her mother and best friend, and now faced caring for her father, who was deteriorating every day. Gail described this time in her life as a gift of both beauty and hardship. She had strong feelings of fear, discomfort, sadness, awkwardness and overwhelming responsibility. She leaned on her faith, praying every day she was making the right decisions for him.

Gail learned to enjoy and appreciate the great moments with her dad and to get through the difficult ones. It was frustrating to get him showered, dressed and carried to his wheelchair to go out to dinner, only to realize 10 minutes later they had to turn around because he needed to go to the bathroom. But Gail just dealt with it. She made the choice not to dwell on the negative things she experienced with her father. If she had a setback, she didn't feel the need to tell everyone how difficult her day had been. She loved her connection with her father. Knowing he had done so much, her labor was one of love.

Gail also learned to enjoy all the happy, present moment experiences she had with her friends and family. She loved to have a nice glass of wine and good conversation and appreciated that even more. Keeping a positive attitude for her father and for herself, Gail took the moment to see love in a friend or in a stranger's eyes, feeling blessed for the joys in her life.

Gail's dad passed away in 2005, after she had cared for him on her own for two and a half years. She was relieved in one way that he wasn't in limbo any longer. She knew her father really enjoyed his life—he loved a good cigar and steak and being with friends—and really fought his death. In fact, three days before he died, he told Gail he would only be around a few more days. He knew it was his time to go.

Gail is an amazing woman and friend who has inspired me with her courage and strength. Whether it's difficult or pleasant, she lives in the moment, and demonstrates the importance of reminding people that you love them every day. You might not get another chance. If you are thinking of someone, leave a voice message or send a note—don't wait! Gail practices this every day. She often leaves me an encouraging voice mail or note when I am going through a challenge or if there is a reason to celebrate. She takes time to recognize both and doesn't expect anything in return. In doing so, she helps me remember that each moment is fleeting . . . and precious.

"We gain strength, and courage, and confidence by each experience in which we really stop to look fear in the face ... we must do that which we think we cannot."

ELEANOR ROOSEVELT

At the Foot of a
GIANT

I met Amy Jones in March of 2009 by phone, when she was just diagnosed with cancer. At the age of 40, she was an author and a seasoned professional speaker with Zig Ziglar. She had just released her book for Simple Truths, *Twice as Much in Half the Time*. Little did everyone know how prophetic her book title would be. It was the most exciting time of her life and the scariest too.

Amy had amazing energy, spirit and faith, with a bubbly personality that was contagious. But her life journey had not been an easy one. She thought she had met the man of her dreams and married him. But the man Amy married chose to walk away from the life he knew, disappearing and abandoning everything in his life, including her. He left messages at his work, for his family, and at their home saying he was taking his life in a "different direction." Amy hired a private investigator, but she realized he was never coming home again. A divorce left her with debt and financial responsibilities, as well as emotional setbacks.

During this very difficult time, Amy started to read Zig Ziglar books to motivate and inspire her. She knew she wanted to work with Zig, but was unsure how. So she set up a time to meet at the Zig Ziglar office for a job. That same day Zig was actually in the office. He met Amy and, after hearing her story of overcoming personal and professional setbacks, immediately knew there was something special about her. The rest was history—Amy went on to tour with Zig for years.

Amy told me that she felt so blessed during this time in her life. She had a career she loved, was amazed to have published a book and had a wonderful loving boyfriend in her life. She felt like everything was going her way. It was almost too good to be true.

Then, after accidently being knocked down on stage at a speaking engagement, Amy experienced a terrible pain in her stomach. She was diagnosed with kidney cancer. The doctors were very aggressive with her cancer, immediately scheduling surgery and starting chemotherapy treatments. She suffered incredible pain while fighting her battle with cancer, and yet still focused on others, even during her last hours.

Amy died on June 2, 2009. I was shocked and brought to tears when I heard the news. I could not believe that I had just spoken to this woman, so full of energy and life, and at the same time so sick. Throughout her life, Amy met each challenge with courage, positively impacting as many people as possible with her stories of over-coming setbacks and her faith in God. Her legacy will outlive her time here on earth. She was a true candle in the wind; a candle that burned out long before her legend ever will.

Tom Ziglar was there during her last moments of life and wrote this incredible story about Amy that I want to share with all of you:

"I will warn you upfront that this is a very difficult post for me to write. My good friend Amy Jones is at the end of her fight against cancer. Sunday night we went to say goodbye. Life is hard.

Sitting in the waiting room talking to Amy's friends and family, brought back so many memories. Just about eight years ago, Amy showed up at our company. All 108 petite pounds of Amy filled the room as her smile and laugh lifted everyone around her. We all fell in love with Amy that day.

As usual, Dad was sitting in the meeting room in the first row, taking notes. When Amy was done, he hugged her and said she needed to be a speaker. Amy's first speech was in front of thousands.

As Amy's speaking career grew, she came on board full-time at Ziglar to spearhead a new program called Ziglar VIP, one of our most successful programs ever. Without Amy, this program would not exist and our company would look much different

today. Amy was our secret weapon—
"Send Amy," we would say. You fall in
love with Amy when you meet her. For
Amy, life is about relationships, so talking
to people about what you believe in is
really just about loving them and understanding their needs. Amy keeps things
pure and simple—I love that about Amy.

Amy and a couple of her friends started
a ministry called the Journey of Sisters.
The Sisters are a group of women who
have overcome incredible tragedies of
all types in their lives. Amy became the
leader, organizing events at homeless
shelters and battered women shelters. More importantly, Amy became the mentor
and coach for the other Sisters. Now there are 14 women in the Journey of Sisters,
every one of them touched by Amy.

As I sat in the waiting room Sunday night reflecting on all of this, Amy continued to
fill the room with her love and grace. The doctors had given her an incredible amount
of pain killers and stimulants so that she would be able to say goodbye. For well
over an hour, Amy spoke God's love into the lives of the 14 Sisters as they gathered

*"Enjoy the little things,
for one day you may look back and realize
they were the big things."*

ROBERT BRAULT

around her bed. She told each one of them the strengths that they possessed and she gave each one of them a charge that was unique to them to carry forward the ministry.

Then it was our turn to see Amy. She told us how much she loved us, and she told Dad what an impact he had on her. We held hands and talked. I teased her, as is my custom, and said, "Amy, 12 disciples was good enough for Jesus, but you needed 14!" She smiled. Somehow, on this incredibly hard day, on this incredibly tough journey, Amy filled everyone with hope and love. Nothing about the goodbye was about Amy. She made it about everyone else. Her peace was perfect and her words were pure.

One of the most difficult things for me these last few months has been how "unfair" this has been. Amy is good, pure, sweet, even fragile in all the right ways. She is someone you want to protect, someone you want to take the place for. She reminds you of Christ, who paid the ultimate price for all of us—pure, innocent, and loving.

On the way out of her room her mother told me, "After everyone leaves tonight they are going to increase her pain medication so that she will no longer suffer. This will allow her to sleep, and when she wakes up, she will be with Jesus."

I realized then that I had not been standing at the bedside of a fragile girl; I had been standing at the foot of a giant."

Amy's book sits on my coffee table in my family room. She is a daily inspiration to me and a reminder that "It's About Time" we all start to live our lives fully. *What are you waiting for?*

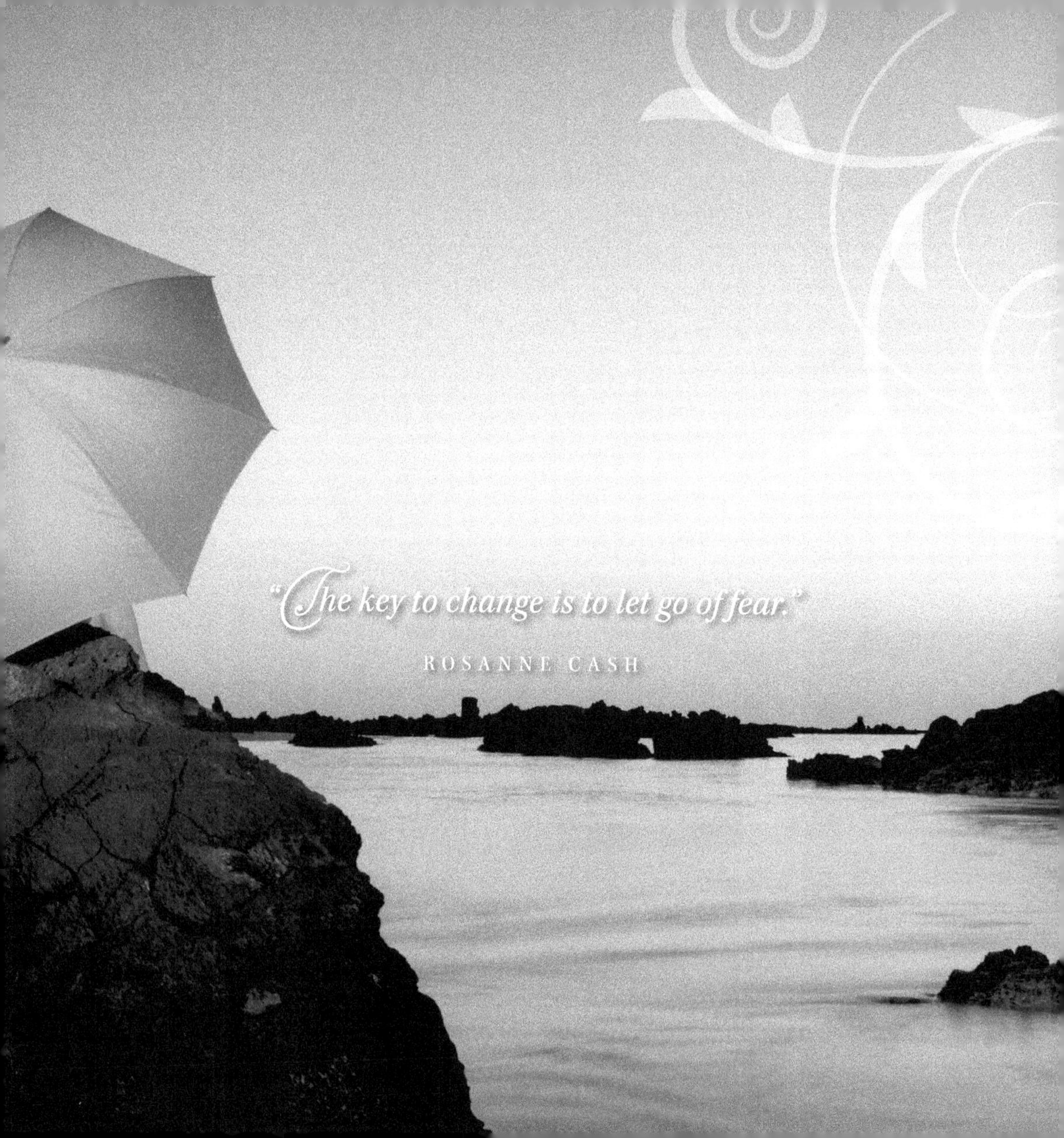

"The key to change is to let go of fear."

ROSANNE CASH

WELCOME
the Rain
~ by Michelle Sedas

As a 12 year-old, I was hospitalized for depression. My desire to be perfect was crippling. Thirteen years later, when I was 25, I found the world too mean and unjust and I felt I had control over nothing. I was, again, hospitalized for depression. This time, however, I was not on the Pediatric Unit. The walls were not bright with painted clouds. We did not make collages of animals nor did we create macaroni pictures. This was real. This was frightening. And this was a place I vowed I would never return.

At a time when I found the world too painful to live in, I was awestruck by some cancer patients' insatiable hunger for life. The irony did not go unnoticed: I was physically healthy, but found myself overwhelmed by the world. I wanted no part in it. On the other hand, many cancer patients possessed such strength and determination to fight their illnesses, while facing the possible reality that their lives may be taken away from them. I wanted to harness their internal passion and find my own hunger for life. I yearned to want to live . . . to find the world a place that I desired to stay in. But I had yet to find the key.

My battle with depression is my own personal rain. This rain came despite my best efforts to prevent it. As heartbreaking as that time was, I am thankful for it because it has given me a richer appreciation and understanding of life. Had I never felt such deep despair, I may have never searched so diligently for ways to overcome negative thinking. And while my faith and relationship with God kept me afloat through the toughest of times, I believe that ultimately He used my depression to help me seek out the key to my happiness: It's not about what happens. It's about perspective. I may not be able to change what takes place, but I can always choose to change my thinking.

I may not be the most organized, the most outgoing, the most confident or the most courageous. But through my journey, I have come to know certain things: I will never be perfect. Our world will never be perfect. *The rain will come, despite my best efforts to prevent it. Life is what you choose to make of it.* State of mind is everything. If you cannot change what happens, then for your happiness, you must change your mindset. In difficult times, remember that this storm will pass. To keep from sinking, find your lifeboat. Just put one foot in front of the other. *Keep breathing. And know that tomorrow the sun will rise.*

"It's not what happens to you,
but how you react to it that matters."

EPICTETUS

Welcome the rain

As the first raindrops fall to the ground
A businessman lets out an angry sigh.
Knowing traffic will be slow, he thinks,
Why me? Why today? Just tell me why!

Outside of town, a farmer scans the horizon
As the storm clouds begin to roll in.
With joy and celebration he calls out,
We are blessed! At last, this drought will end!

In every life storms will come:
Adversity, Inconvenience, or Pain.
Only we can choose how we will respond:
To be overwhelmed or to Welcome the Rain.

It's not about what happens to us.
It's what we think, internalize, and perceive.
It's not about the external events.
It's what we choose to believe.

Believe the difficult times help us grow.
They build character, strength and wisdom.
Believe life's challenges can truly be blessings.
And with this understanding comes freedom ...

For we're no longer at the mercy of the wind,
Being forcefully tossed around.
When we can see life through different eyes
The world's joys and beauties abound.

So as you continue on life's journey,
And feel the presence of rain's first dew,
Stand strong, be determined, remain focused.
And remember what is so true:

When we choose to see beyond life's storms
A new perspective we will gain
Since we will only find our rainbow
After we ... Welcome the Rain

"Each time we face our fear, we gain strength, courage, and confidence in the doing."

UNKNOWN

STAY FOCUSED
on your vision

Life can take you in unexpected directions — sometimes in ways you definitely wouldn't choose. If you stick to your vision and your values, you can find a greater purpose.

For my friends Tammy and Tom, it was love at first sight. It took just a few dates for them to know that they had each found their soul mate. They married and had two beautiful children. Both were busy professionals, but if the phone rang and it was an important issue for the family, they were there for each other.

After their children were born, Tom started his own business conducting leadership conferences. He was a naturally gifted leader and speaker and had a passion for inspiring and teaching others. For him, having a business that fostered relationships was a dream come true.

As the company grew, Tom hired one of his best friends, David. Tom's philosophy was if you were going to have great business success, financially and professionally, you might as well enjoy the journey with your friends and family. Both Tom and David were extreme sports enthusiasts who enjoyed water skiing, snow skiing and mountain biking.

On a 4th of July vacation, Tom and Tammy's lives changed in an instant. Tom and David were mountain biking when Tom's front bike tire hit a rock, flipping him over the front of his bike and breaking his neck. Tom was only 51 years old when he died.

This was something Tammy never expected. Why did this happen to Tom? He was a great athlete and did crazy things, but always landed on his feet. Tammy was conservative and thoughtful about the decisions she made. This tragedy was absolutely devastating and didn't make any sense. She and Tom had a strong Christian faith, and she knew she would have to lean on her faith in God because she was not prepared to face this journey alone.

Tammy was suddenly thrown into the role of being a single parent and the CEO of a multi-million dollar company. She started contacting sponsors and attendees, assuring them that she was fine and very capable of continuing Tom's work and vision.

Tammy was strong for her children and for everyone working at the company, but didn't have much time to think about herself; the tasks at hand were immense and needed attention. Her courage came from staying true to the life vision she and Tom had created together. She successfully ran the business before selling it, executing a deal that relieved her from the day-to-day business and allowed her to focus on her children and the children's foundation that she started with Tom.

Tammy continued Tom's legacy by working on some of the projects he started including a book and movie idea. She also expanded their children's foundation to include a high school charity basketball tournament that teaches teens the importance of giving back to their communities. After only two years, this basketball tournament grew to be the largest in the United States with more than 250 college coaches attending and offering scholarships to players.

With such overwhelming responsibilities in such a short time, Tammy could easily have become paralyzed with fear. But she wasn't afraid to ask for help if she needed it. Waking up each day to the reality that Tom was no longer there took her a long time to accept, and is a reminder to enjoy every precious day with her family and friends.

Tammy tells her story with grace and confidence, knowing that she is driven by a higher faith and bigger purpose. She has an amazing spirit and energy that is immediately contagious. Tom and Tammy believed that because life blessed them with success, it was important for them to help others. Together, they knew the importance of believing in their dreams and pursuing them with a vengeance.

*"In the midst of winter,
I found there was an invincible me in the summer."*

ALBERT CAMUS

CHRISTOPHER'S GIFTS—
the Tale of Two Quilts
~ By Radha Stern

If you had to pick one word to describe me—it would be "mother." I am the person who hears "mom" in a grocery store and turns around, the one who opens my door to all friends and family and enjoys bringing them into my home and nurturing them. But a tragic event challenged my devotion to mothering. My son, Christopher Robin Hotchkiss, was murdered nearly 14 years ago. As a mother, I wanted to put the band-aid on, give the kisses and make everything fine again. This time, band-aids and kisses would not work.

I was making lunch for my brother and a friend when I received the news from the sheriff that my 21-year-old son had been shot and killed by his roommate. I had just seen

Christopher a few days earlier. He came to visit and I'd stocked him up with enough food for the week. We did his laundry together and when he left he gave me a huge hug and told me, "I love you, Mom," as his green eyes sparkled.

Shock set in. My body rocked back and forth. I kept saying, "They killed him." I cried rivers of tears. The shock was so much more physical than I'd ever imagined. I felt like I had been run over by a huge tractor trailer truck, without visible bruises or breaks. I was racked with emotions. It all seemed unreal, like a horror movie. But this was VERY REAL!

I realized very quickly our chapter with Christopher in it was over. I wouldn't watch him get married, wouldn't be a grandmother to his children. Our photo albums would not be filled by him and our lives would never be the same. No more memories with Christopher in them. Could this really be?

It is hard to remember everything that day. I did sleep; sleep was a safe place for me to be with my sorrow. I didn't know if I would ever smile again, be happy, feel pleasure or even be able to walk into a room full of people. The violence of Christopher's death—he was shot with a handgun four times—made it more difficult.

The next morning, I awoke to waves of grief rolling into my body and soul. My tears could have filled an ocean. I was still in shock. I would go outside just to feel the cold, so I could sense where my body ended.

My "Mother on Earth," Beth, (my biological mother died three days after Christopher was born) said, "You don't have to get over this, ever." That was a comforting thing to hear ... and still is to this day. I was relieved that people did not expect me to "get over" the death of my son. Why would I want to ever "get over" him? He is part of me.

When he heard the news of Christopher's death, another friend told me, "Radha, don't let this man take any more from you. He has taken more than he was ever entitled to. Don't move; go on vacation—LIVE—don't let this man take more from your life and the life of your family."

This was the first time in my life I was not taking care of everyone else. I was the doer in our family, the glue that bound us together. Now it was someone else's turn. I felt the need to give the tragedy of Christopher's murder my full focus and energy. I arranged grounding things for myself, regular massages and short visits with close friends. It was a time I needed to be kind to myself and not feel selfish for doing what I needed to do to get through another day. I learned that the shower and the treadmill were great places to cry, and I realized I had permission to cry anywhere at any time for the rest of my life.

It was a difficult time, coming to grips with the fact that the rest of the world was turning as usual. People drove to work and shopped for dinner while our world was turned upside down. Would life ever be normal again? What was normal? The first time I went into my local grocery store to buy food I remember thinking, "Don't all you people know how much pain I am in?" I realized, of course not. They did not have a clue.

We held a memorial service for Christopher and scattered his ashes on Mt. Tamalpais, where he loved to watch the sunset, under a beautiful and majestic California Bay Tree.

I joined Compassionate Friends two weeks later, a grief group for parents who have lost children. It was very hard for me to walk into the room for my first meeting,

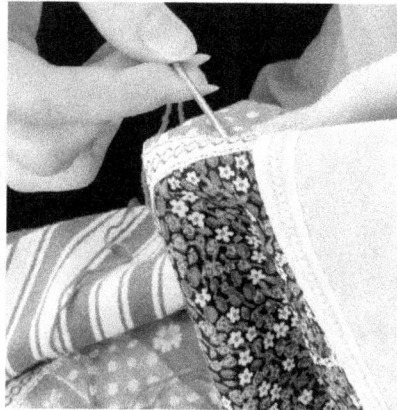

"Forgiveness is the fragrance that the violet sheds on the heel that has crushed it."

MARK TWAIN

though it was good for me not to feel so alone. I took my daughter, Christina, to the meetings with me. It was important to me to include her in everything I did to help with grieving. I also started volunteering with the Trauma Foundation, part of San Francisco General Hospital, to work on gun control.

By Fall 1997, I was gearing up for "the biggest job of my life"—the trial for which our family had waited 18 months. After enduring five weeks in a courtroom, we had a verdict: Mark James Taylor was convicted of second degree murder and sentenced to 19 ½ years to life.

After several months passed, I began to jump back into life, looking ahead for the first time since Christopher was murdered. I commissioned a quilt by a local artist, Liz Piatt, to capture the special events in Christopher's life, including a heart for each of Christopher's 21 years.

Liz called me to get the quilt on the day before what would have been Christopher's 25th birthday. Family and friends went with me for the showing. Everyone gasped when they saw Christopher's quilt, and then happy tears started to flow. The quilt hangs in my bedroom, where I wake up to it every day.

At Christmas in 2003, I met Jacques Verduin, a clinical psychologist, who asked if I would be willing to work with him on the Insight Prison Project. He wanted to understand the effects of murder on people and their families, believing this was a missing part of his education in working with prisoners. After several sessions with Jacques, I was ready to go to San Quentin to share my story with prisoners in a group called Katargeo, a Greek word meaning "freedom from that which binds you."

Over the course of an hour, I slowly told 17 prisoners my story of Christopher, sharing photos and personal tales. As I spoke, I looked at each person's face around the circle. When I finished, I was in a room full of men who were not just crying, but openly sobbing. I was moved by their reactions; in fact, I was overwhelmed. These men realized they had created this type of pain for a family, and everyone connected to that family. It is the "pebble in the pond" effect, the ripples far reaching. The prisoners saw the pain I live with every day without my son—and all of them live every day with the knowledge and pain of having taken a person's life.

On one of my visits to Katargeo, I brought Christopher's quilt into the prison, telling the story of the quilt and how it came to be. After this, I continued working with the group, even preparing a home cooked Thanksgiving meal for the men.

As the 10th anniversary of Chris' death approached in 2006, I went to see the Katargeo men at San Quentin, and they shared how significant they felt it had been to work with me over the past three years.

One man said, "You taught me that you shouldn't get upset about the small stuff. I killed my friend because he owed me money. That should have never bothered me like it did."

I cried softly and asked myself, "Me? I taught him that?"

Another man said, "I only have one word for you . . . Grace." I was in tears and I was humbled. We don't get the opportunity to see how the steps we take in life reverberate through others' lives, and here were 17 men telling me I made a difference in theirs. This was a true gift.

Then one of the prisoners said, "We have a gift for you." I was surprised. I was already taken aback by their generosity. A large white garbage bag was put gently on my lap and as I opened it, a quilt revealed itself. These men had made a quilt about Christopher! Two men held the quilt so I could read each square—18 quilt pieces mounted on a large piece of black felt. All the materials came from somewhere in the prison. Fabric from a mattress, a handkerchief, a section of a shirt, even leather from the hobby shop were all part of the quilt. I wept, emotionally overwhelmed and grateful for this poignant sharing.

Since the day of Christopher's death in 1996, I had been working on "finding comfort" . . . a place in my soul and spirit where I can be peaceful with the tragic event of murder. I found part of it in a very strange place—San Quentin.

For almost seven years, I have been working with a number of the men in San Quentin, helping them to come to terms with all the consequences of crime. One thing I know for certain: Christopher's death does not mean my death. I live fully for my family and friends here on earth, and in that way I honor my son. He might not be here in body, but he's here in many other ways.

I want to honor the process of grieving, to hold my heart open, to follow this journey to where it has taken and will take me. And I will always be thankful that I was able to mother my son, Christopher, for his short life on earth.

"*There is no education like adversity.*"

DISRAELI

A Woman's
WHEELS

~ *By Cathy Conheim*

Chris Timmins is an amazing woman. Twenty-six years ago, she and her husband were preparing to leave San Diego and move to Oregon. On a bright, sunny morning, while they were finishing up last-minute details, Chris was feeling nostalgic and decided to take one last spin around Fiesta Island in her beloved little BMW convertible. What happened to her on that drive is still a bit of a mystery. Was it the hot sun? Was it fatigue? What was it that caused her to black out while driving? She could feel herself losing consciousness, and tried to pull over to the side of the road. But she lost control and crashed into a cement road divider. When she regained consciousness in the hospital, she was a quadriplegic. Her whole life was turned upside down.

Chris's husband left her about four years later. She lost her job as a school teacher and had to fight for the next year to get it back. She also spent the next two years battling with the State of California to get them to pay for a handicapped van that would allow her to drive. Such a van cost $75,000 in those days—an impossible amount for a woman who had just lost her life as she had known it.

Her health challenges weren't over, either. Thirteen years later, Chris was struck with breast cancer.

She not only rose to meet each of these personal and professional crises, she triumphed over them. Chris was finally able to convince the San Diego School District that her presence in the classroom would greatly enrich the education of her students. Her message to the kids: "It's not the events of your life that determine the kind of future you'll have. It's how you respond to those events that gives you quality in your life." Chris was, and is, the living embodiment of that message.

Chris was able to get her special van from the State—her Freedom Van—which gave her the ability to go to work every day, to be out and about like millions of other mobile southern Californians. And she found a physician, Dr. Donna, who would see to Chris' unique medical needs over the years.

I've been friends with Chris for more than 20 years. I've always been impressed with her pluck and optimism, in the face of tragedies, struggles, and losses that would have done in a lesser woman.

Last year, Chris hit a final roadblock, and this one she just didn't know how to overcome. Her van was now 20 years old and just about worn out. The state program only provides one van per person in their lifetime. And today, a specially equipped van for a person who has to drive using her head costs $115,000. How could a single woman, on a school teacher's salary, afford such an expensive vehicle? If she could no longer drive, she would have to quit her job just seven years shy of retirement. Chris had no idea what to do. For the first time, it seemed that this breaking-down hunk of metal was going to be the last straw.

One day Chris and I were talking about her predicament. It seemed like such a dumb problem. After all she'd been through, this ancient van was going to stop her? I just couldn't accept that. "This is ridiculous," I told her. "We're just gonna get you a new van."

"But how?" Chris asked.

"Never mind how," I told her. "We're just going to go buy the van tomorrow and we'll figure out how to pay for it later!"

And so we did. We did some research and found that the van she needed had to be a 2003 model, because the 2004 model had a gas tank in it that prohibited it from being modified for a handicapped-accessible vehicle. We found that there were only seven such vans left in the entire state. So we found a dealer who had one, and we bought it. Our small private foundation, of which I am a trustee, put up $40,000 for a deposit on the van. Normally we give just small cash grants of $500 to $1,000 to people in emergencies, but this case seemed to merit more. Chris had done so much in her life to help herself, but this time she needed help from others.

That was Labor Day, and by Christmas we had raised the rest of the money all by e-mail! Here's how we did it: We sent out 50 e-mails to people we knew, people who trusted us. We explained the situation and told them, "We promise you that every cent you send us will go to pay for the van. Not a penny will go to administration, not even postage!" We also asked them to go one step further: "Send this e-mail to 10 people you know who trust you. Make the same promise to them that we made to you, and request that they pass along the request to ten more people who trust them." We were building a community of trust. There are so many fund-raising scams out there; we needed for people to trust us and to trust one another.

We kept our promise and they kept theirs. For the first two weeks, we received checks from people we knew. But by the third week, we stared getting money from people whose names we didn't recognize. The network was working, and our community of trust was doing its job.

What made this feat all the more remarkable is that it happened at a time when the San Diego area was ravaged by the worst wildfires in our history. It was a terrible time to try to be raising money. People were feeling helpless and hopeless in the face of such a community disaster. This is a common problem—people get so overwhelmed in the face of others' needs, that they often do nothing. They think, "What can I do? I'm just one person." They don't think that one person can make a difference or that what they have to offer counts.

Our story is bigger than just getting a new Freedom Van for Chris. It's the story of showing people that they can make a difference, even if it's just sending in $1, or $5 or $10. We got a lot of small contributions in those months. We didn't need a big important wealthy donor—we just needed lots of individuals, regular folks, to give what they could. Our project had the same message of Chris' entire life: We are NOT paralyzed as people—there is always something we can do, no matter how big the problem. By taking action, any action, people can overcome their own personal sense of paralysis.

We didn't need one person to give us $70,000—we would have been happier to get 70,000 people to give just $1 each. People are glad to be part of something that makes a difference. If everybody picked just one other person to help, the world would be transformed.

Our next project is transforming that dumb law that says each disabled person can only have one state-sponsored van in their lifetime. *Anyone want to join us in making a difference with that?*

(For further information, contact Cathy Conheim at www.realwomenproject.org)

"*Be strong and courageous!*
Don't be afraid or discouraged . . .
for there is a power far greater on our side!
We have the Lord our God to help us and
to fight our battles for us!"

II CHRONICLES 32:7-8 (NLT)

$\mathcal{I}$ had the pleasure of meeting Paula Fox when I was just beginning to write this book. She was very encouraging to me at a time when all I had was a vision and a passion for this topic. She agreed to contribute a poem and her poem captured it perfectly——the quiet strength and courage these women possess. I want to share it with you as you go through your daily challenges and need a little encouragement.

COURAGE

doesn't always roar...

BY PAULA FOX

When life gets you down and the problems you face
are certainly more than your share ...
When you run out of strength and you want to give up
because it's just too much to bear ...

I want to remind you, my precious friend,
that you have what it takes inside ...
extraordinary courage that may not ROAR
but it doesn't cower and hide.

It's the quiet voice inside you that says,
"Tomorrow I'll try again."
It's the courage to keep on going . . .
to see things through to the end.

You are not *defined by this moment in time.*
You are not *what has happened to you.*
It's the way that you choose to respond that matters
and what you decide to do.

Courage is not the absence of fear,
but a powerful choice we make.
It's the choice to move forward with PURPOSE *and joy,*
regardless of what it takes.

It's the courage that's found in ordinary women
who are HEROES in their own way...
exhibiting strength and fortitude
in life's challenges every day...

Valiant women of exceptional courage
with enduring power to cope...
taking each problem one day at a time
and never giving up HOPE.

These brave-hearted women have great resilience
and they lift each other as well...
bonded by a common understanding,
each with a story to tell.

We're encouraged by the faith of others
to survive and overcome.
We have courage to say,

*"I may be down...
but the battle is not done!"*

For the WOMAN of COURAGE is a winner
regardless of what she loses.
She displays amazing beauty and strength
with the attitude she chooses.

She gives herself the permission she needs
to feel disappointed or sad.
But then she empowers herself with FAITH ...
to focus on good things... not bad.

She develops a greater *compassion* for others

as she sees with wide open eyes.

She reaches new levels of *empathy* ...

much more understanding and wise.

Her story is one of gentle *strength*

reminding us all once more ...

Steel is sometimes covered in velvet,

and ...

COURAGE doesn't always roar!

"*Courage is the ladder on which all virtues mount.*"

CLARE BOOTH LUCE

Just the Right
ATTITUDE

Debra W. South Jones knows first-hand what it's like to struggle, but she also knows how to turn a tough situation into a solution—one that allows thousands to go to bed at night with a full stomach.

A mother in her 30s who was fighting ovarian and thyroid cancer, Debra had to retire from her accounting job. That left her in a catch-22. After her first husband left her, she didn't make enough money to feed her son and daughter, but was told she made too much to qualify for food stamps. So she survived on disability checks and help from family and friends.

"I felt so humiliated," she said.

She promised God that if she got better she would find a way to help people who were hungry and struggling. From that promise, and a few shelves of canned goods,

grew a United Way agency, Just The Right Attitude (JTRA), that now doles out hope and 2.5 million pounds of food a year.

Established in 1999, JTRA quickly expanded its outreach, providing food for 850 families out of Debra's converted one-car garage. But, because of a neighbor's complaint, her operation was going to be shut down.

Debra turned to her community again for support and a local car dealer, Troy Duhon, heard her call. He had seen a news report about her project's grand opening, and offered Debra the top floor of one of his dealerships. By 2003, JTRA was serving 4,000 families a month. When Katrina struck two years later, demand doubled.

Before it became too late to leave, Debra evacuated to Atlanta. Later, she learned that everything she had left behind—her car, home and personal belongings—were gone. Troy Duhon lost everything too.

But Debra was no stranger to struggle, so she set her mind to rebuilding her life and the food bank. For 18 months, Debra lived at her mother's in Breaux Bridge, over 200 miles from New Orleans. Each day began at 4:45 a.m., as she drove three-and-a-half hours one-way in a car that a friend gave her. For the first two months, she worked out of a gutted dealership. When Troy began rebuilding, she moved to the parking lot of a church across the street.

JTRA consisted of two big tents and four storage pods. One tent morphed into a drive-through food bank, serving 26,000 families a month, while the second tent housed a makeshift kitchen. Four small generators fueled rice cookers and electric skillets, while large pots of beans simmered on a two-burner propane stove. Sixteen thousand families received a hot breakfast and lunch every month. In cold weather, generator-run heaters warmed the volunteers while they worked. The operation was nothing fancy, but it became a lifeline for struggling families—one day, one meal, at a time.

While I was working in New Orleans last year, I met Debra and learned more about her food bank. More than three years after Katrina struck the Gulf Coast, *Just The Right Attitude* still serves 15,000 families every month. The food bank continues to be filled by Second Harvest and other donors, but demand still outstrips supply. JTRA regularly runs food drives to fill the gaps. And because of Debra's promise to help anyone who asks, JTRA has received no governmental support of any kind.

Despite her cancers, a series of strokes and heart attacks, knee surgery and chronic back pain, Debra South Jones is full of energy and at work every day. Athletes learn to push through the pain for the duration of a race or a game, and so does Debra. She is an inspiration to many in her community—an unsung hero, who perseveres through every challenge. With an unstoppable "bring it on attitude," Debra's courageous actions have been the driving force in helping to feed thousands of people, a one-woman solution to attacking hunger in her corner of the world.

"*Fall seven times, stand up eight.*"

JAPANESE PROVERB

A MOTHER'S COURAGE

~ By Linda Kramer Jenning

Every morning, Becky Ziegel gets anxious. Just before ten, sitting at her kitchen counter with a cup of coffee, she tries to concentrate on the day ahead. But her eyes keep drifting to the cell phone at her elbow. Where is the text message from Ty?

"If I don't hear from him," she says, "it's panic time. I'll call him, and if he doesn't answer, I'm in my car. I'll drive over to his house with my heart pounding so hard, I can feel it in my neck."

Now a chiming sound signals a new message, and Becky's shoulders relax as she reads it: "Brain and bodily functions seem to be working as 'normally' as possible." She can head upstairs to her sewing room knowing that her son made it through another night.

"I'd be dead if my parents weren't within driving distance," says Tyler Ziegel, who is 26 and lives in his own place about ten miles from his family's home in Metamora, Illinois. Ty, a former Marine, is officially retired from the military, with disability compensation for the massive injuries he sustained in a suicide bombing in western Iraq. He lost part of his left arm and right hand, most of his face, and a piece of his brain. Today, he has recovered enough to function without constant care, but seizures and other health problems have sent him to the ER four times in recent months.

In 2006, two years after he was wounded, Ty wed his hometown sweetheart, Renee Kline, to whom he had proposed between his two deployments to Iraq. But the marriage unraveled, and the couple divorced after a year. Since then, Becky, like thousands of mothers of disabled vets, has been her son's main caregiver. While Ty credits his whole family and his friends for rallying around him, he singles her out. "My mom has been awesome," he says. "She's been there for me through everything."

"I unloaded him, and now he's back," Becky says, laughing. She drives him to appointments at the Veterans Affairs clinic in nearby Peoria and the VA hospital more than two hours away in Danville. She makes sure he eats well and takes his medications. She helps him with the housecleaning and bill paying. And, of course, she checks every morning that her son is still breathing.

"I'm the mom," she says. "This is what I do."

Becky is 49 and the mother of two Marines, both of whom joined up after high school. Ty shipped out to Iraq for his second tour in the summer of 2004, shortly after his little brother, Zach, left for boot camp. With both boys gone, Becky admits, she "did the happy dance." She and her husband, Jeff, 56, a heavy-equipment operator, finally had an empty nest. "I was thinking, they're grown; they don't need me anymore. Who do I want to be?" She considered taking some college classes; she planned to visit friends she hadn't seen in years.

One day in December, Ty was on patrol in Anbar province when an Iraqi insurgent detonated a carload of explosives beside the convoy's troop truck. Of the seven men on board, Ty took the hardest hit. A buddy pulled him out and smothered the flames. Ty was evacuated to a military hospital at Balad Air Base, where surgeons worked to save his life.

Becky was getting ready to wrap Christmas presents when a Marine officer called with the news. When Jeff handed her the phone, she didn't cry but pumped the officer for information. He could offer little more than a sketchy description of the attack and Ty's injuries.

From Balad, Ty was flown 17 hours to Brooke Army Medical Center in San Antonio, Texas. The Fisher House Foundation—a national nonprofit that aids and temporarily houses the families of wounded soldiers—arranged for plane tickets for Becky and Jeff, along with Ty's fiancée, Renee, and Zach, who was just home on leave. They got to Brooke on Christmas Eve.

A neurologist filled them in on Ty's condition. Surgeons at Balad had removed the shrapnel-pierced part of his left frontal lobe. It was too soon to know if his mental capability or his personality would be altered, if he would be paralyzed, if he'd even wake up at all. Everything above his waist was severely burned. "They really didn't expect him to make it," says Becky.

When the family entered Ty's room, they found him wrapped in bandages with a tube protruding from his head. "We couldn't see his face," Becky recalls. "But his legs poked out, and I could see the crossed-rifles tattoo. That's how I knew it was Ty."

After Ty survived the first critical weeks, his father and brother flew back to Metamora. Becky and Renee stayed behind, moving into a suite at the local Fisher House. The women rotated shifts at Ty's bedside. They fed him and helped him shower. They stretched his remaining two fingers—both badly burned—to increase their range of motion. "I remember days I'd think, I can't walk in that room and put on a happy face," Becky says. "I don't know how I did it. I just did. My kid."

That May, Jeff came to visit and brought Becky a ring with three diamonds—past, present, and future—to celebrate their 25th wedding anniversary. They strolled on San Antonio's River Walk and took in the sights. Becky had been living at Fisher House for five months. One more anniversary would come and go before she got back home.

She'd never spent much time away from the patch of country outside Peoria where she was raised. She married Jeff at 20, and they bought her grandparents' old house, which is still her home.

"I never could have imagined living somewhere else and not having family and friends around," she says. But her 19 months in San Antonio opened up "the little box" of her world. "Now I can go anywhere and make friends and find family."

Becky was delighted to see Ty moving toward independence. Aside from headaches, he showed no signs of lasting brain damage. With Ty making progress, Becky took some time for herself. She walked for miles on a track near the hospital. On the "your-son-getting-blown-up-diet," she shed 60 pounds. She let her short blonde perm grow shoulder-length and dyed it auburn.

"I was finding me," Becky recalls. "I felt better about myself." She even began doing public speaking to raise support for Fisher House. Then finally, in July 2006, Ty and Becky headed home.

After Ty got married, his mother enrolled in the college courses she'd looked forward to for so long. Even after Ty and Renee separated, Becky held on to her new freedom. Ty stayed in the white clapboard bungalow he'd lived in with his wife. He'd been diagnosed with post-traumatic stress disorder, but medication helped lessen his anxiety.

Zach sent an e-mail to Becky from Iraq, where he'd been deployed the previous fall: "What was God thinking? Why does all this stuff have to be happening to us?"

Becky typed back, "Because we can handle it."

Sometimes—not often—she feels almost overwhelmed by the hand life has dealt her, and she worries. "What if something happens? What if I don't get there in time? It scares the hell out of me." She finds comfort, though, in her circle of loved ones and her "second family" of wounded vets and their parents. She tries not to dwell on what she can't change.

"Ty asked me once if I was angry about what happened to him," Becky says. "But who would I be angry at? The bomber? He's dead. Ty? I'm proud of him. I couldn't pick anybody to be angry at, so I wasn't angry."

Her studies on hold, job offers let go, Becky fully expects to pick up where she left off sometime in the future. She imagines the day when Ty will need her less, even marry again. "The woman who ends up with him is going to be lucky," she says. "I can't wait till he has his own kids.

"I don't expect to be at Ty's beck and call for the rest of my life," she adds, curling up on the sofa where her son often sleeps. "But you're never done being the mom."

Excerpted from Readers Digest.com June 2009.

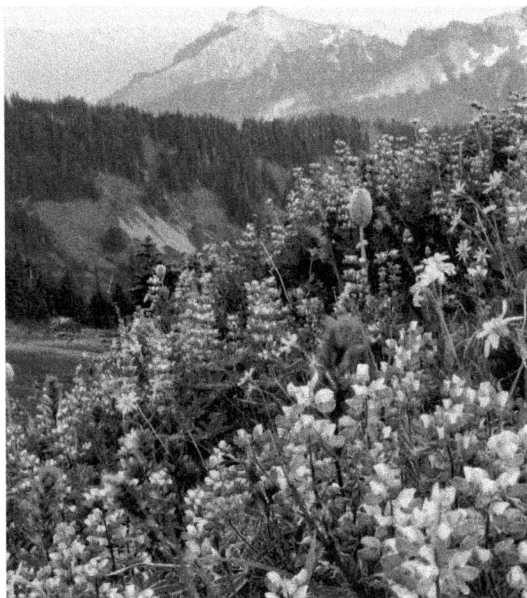

*"We must have courage to bet on our ideas, to take
the calculated risk, and to act. Everyday living requires
courage if life is to be effective and bring happiness."*

MAXWELL MALTZ

"*You* must be the change you wish to see in the world."

GHANDI

Overcoming Anger With
FORGIVENESS

It took a young woman's experience from halfway around the world to help me move past the anger I felt after my parents' accident. In the book, *Left to Tell,* Immaculee Ilibagiza tells the most heart-wrenching story of courage. Growing up in a small village in Rwanda with her parents and her three brothers, Immaculee had just entered college in 1994, when the genocide of the Tutsis occurred.

When Hutu rebels took over the government, Immaculee witnessed some of the most horrific crimes—some committed by men who were friends of her family. At this time, Immaculee was separated from her parents and brothers. She was saved by a local minister who hid her and seven other women in his bathroom for 91 days. The women could not leave and could barely move. They were occasionally fed scraps from the trash because the minister didn't want any of the household staff to become suspicious and turn him in to the Hutus for hiding Tutsis.

Immaculee prayed constantly to save her and her family from this horrible terror. She often heard friends outside the bathroom window talking about killing all Tutsi cockroaches and saying terrible things about her own family.

Immaculee focused on getting out of the situation alive and she began to develop a vision for the future. While still hidden at the minister's house, she realized that she would need to learn English. A goal began to form: She wanted to work for the United Nations in order to help others and prevent this tragedy from ever happening again. Immaculee asked the minister if he had any books in English. Her days were filled with praying and learning English, all while gunfire and bloodshed happened all around her.

Finally after 91 days, the French army came to the minister's house and released the women, but their journey was not over. The women were so weak and malnourished from being cramped in such a small space for months that they could barely walk. They were transferred to a safe French camp and then transported in the back of a truck to the next safe zone. The truck only made it halfway to their destination. In the heart of the Hutu rebels, the women were told they had to get out and walk two miles to the next safe camp. They thought they were doomed—they had made it this far only to be killed by the rebels. But Immaculee had a plan and she knew with confidence that it was not her time to die.

Miraculously, they made it to safety and Immaculee was given a second chance to continue her education and live her life. She discovered that only one of her brothers survived; the rest of her family was brutally murdered. Immaculee went on to fulfill her dream . . . and more. She graduated, moved to the U.S., got a job with the U.N., married a wonderful man and has two children.

Years later, she had the opportunity to return to her Rwandan hometown. She traveled to the place where her family home had been burnt and wept at the loss and devastation that genocide had caused not only her family, but her country. While she was there, she wanted to visit the prison where the murderer of her mom and brother was being kept.

The officer brought a prisoner in to see her, an older man in handcuffs—the man who had brutally murdered her mother and brother and who wanted to kill her as well. Immaculee was surprised to find the man was once a successful and handsome Hutu businessman whose kids she had played with in primary school. Now, he was a disheveled, limping old man who could not look her in the face. The officer told her she could do or say whatever she wanted to this man. Immaculee felt an overwhelming return of the anger and hatred she had lived with for so many years. But, her faith in God and humanity gave her the freedom to move beyond the anger. She looked the man straight in the eyes and with great courage told him, "I forgive you." The man was shocked and so was the officer who immediately removed him and asked Immaculee, "How could you ever forgive this man?"

In forgiving her worst enemy, Immaculee focused on the loving spirit she found in her faith and in others, rather than on hatred and anger. She is a role model and source of inspiration for me. After my parents' accident, I felt extremely angry and wanted the man who hit them not only to go to jail, but also to be punished for the rest of his life. I became obsessed with seeking revenge. Some days I was so angry, I wished someone would just provoke an argument with me so I could unleash all my pent-up anger on them. I felt lost, depressed and angry at God for letting this happen to my family and me. I knew I had to find a different path—one that allowed me to move forward, forgive and find happiness in the present moment and in the journey I shared with my mother. I just didn't know how.

After finding a counselor, I started to read some self-help books. One that had great impact on me was, *Why Bad Things Happen to Good People* by Rabbi Kushner. After reading the book, I was able to better understand my relationship with God as well as my struggles with my own personal experience. I knew that I could no longer let this horrible experience identify me. With a new perspective, I learned to move past my anger in order to follow my bigger purpose on earth.

I cannot imagine anyone going through more than Immaculee Ilibagiza. Her story is one of hope and inspiration, of perseverance and courage. Just as Immaculee so eloquently tells in her story, God had another plan for me as well.

How do you spell Courage?

BY BJ GALLAGHER

CREATE a brave new world for yourself.

OPEN your mouth and speak your truth.

UNMASK bullies and cowards.

REPEL fear.

ACKNOWLEDGE your own inner strength.

GET into action.

EMBRACE faith as your source.

"*We could never learn to be brave and patient if there were only joy in the world.*"

HELEN KELLER

A Second
CHANCE

~ By Donna Dennison

A lengthy stay in the ICU brought a frequent comment by health care professionals, "You are lucky to be alive. Aren't you glad you have been given a second chance?" Days were spent thinking about this question, wondering how I should respond.

Somewhere in the space between life and death, I didn't feel trapped. I wasn't really scared. It was as if life on earth was suspended, while the ravages of cancer and its ugly side effects battled against God's will for my life. At the time, I waited, not really aware of how close I came to leaving this Earth. Now, I am acutely aware of the renewed opportunity for life that I've been granted.

EVERY day, I am given a second chance. It has less to do with another near-death experience as with the choices and decisions I make and my interactions with others. Some of these are conscious choices, while others seem to flow with the pace of the day.

Where do I go from here? I have months of healing ahead. There are still many unknowns, and a continued focus on my physical being. My life will be surrounded by health care professionals, all with their own opinions about how to best heal my body. While my physical body has much to do with being able to fulfill my dreams and passions, I can now build a life based upon:

1. *Rest.* My dear friend, Mary Anne, calls rest the ultimate elixir and says it takes a profound shift to embrace napping as an accomplishment! Rest and napping? I used to think these were a waste of time and others would view me as being lazy. My body says rest, I rest. To do otherwise will compromise my return to good health!

2. *Repair.* Time spent repairing the body parts ravaged by infection and cancer is a continued priority. Time spent in the present must take priority over dreams of the future. My future is RIGHT NOW, this moment, on this day.

3. *Respect.* I haven't always respected my own uniqueness and my role in this world. I put too much emphasis on what others think. I judged myself by my physical appearance and always fell short. At the edge of life, it didn't matter that tumors had changed my wrist and hip into vehicles of pain. It was frustrating not to have a voice, but I never lost my words. It didn't matter that all the drugs and fluids caused a 20-pound weight gain. It didn't matter that

my hair lost its luster; that my eyes were bright with pain and infection instead of life. What matters is my breath, my heart song, and my belief in things greater and grander than me!

4. *Renewal.* I have a unique chance to begin each day anew. What I do with the day is primarily up to me. Doctors' appointments and tests will prioritize my time, but nothing prevents my heart and soul from continuing toward a renewed spirit of service to self and others.

5. *Rejoicing.* It is hard to find the humor in illness … to think of those silly moments that make me bend over in hysterical laughter. Yet, each day has moments that are silly and outrageous, ones filled with the cuteness of life. I realize time and again these are wonderfully defining moments of my day, if I pay attention.

No matter if I have been given one day or many years, I have a second chance, each and every day. I have the capability, the perseverance, and the diligence to see another day … far grander and greater than the previous one. Each day is overflowing with the capacity to fill me with love, gratitude and compassion for myself and others.

Life: how great thou art.

I'm here!

"*Courage is the capacity to confront
what can be imagined.*"

LEO C. ROSTEN

A Special Birth of
LOVE *and*
COURAGE

Kyle and Logan are two now. The birth of these twin boys is a story of love and courage. It begins, as all stories do, with their parents—my good friends Vera and Dave. Vera met Dave when she was 41 years old. She knew she had found the right man to marry.

After their wedding, they wanted to get pregnant as soon as possible, which is exactly what happened. Unfortunately, just a few weeks after confirming her pregnancy, Vera experienced a miscarriage, her first of three. She then began fertility treatments, which were unsuccessful for three years. While they both wanted to have a child together, Vera and Dave never thought they would experience so many setbacks and disappointments.

The hormones started taking a toll on Vera's self-esteem and energy level. She felt like a different woman than the one Dave had married. Her focus on getting pregnant had surpassed everything else in her life. Vera always had a vision of having her own child and began questioning why she had waited so long to get married.

Finally, at 44, Vera thought it may not be in her future to have children of her own. She came to peace with this and accepted the reality. Vera and Dave started to focus on adoption. The day Vera was supposed to fly to Montenegro in Southeastern Europe to adopt a baby, it all fell through.

"Kind words can be short and easy to speak, but their echoes are truly endless."

MOTHER TERESA

Adopting a baby in the United States posed its own special problems. As Canadian citizens working and living in the United States, they would have to move back to Canada in order to adopt. Since Dave's job was in the U.S., it was not an easy change. Feeling let down once again, Vera decided it was not meant for her to adopt a child either.

Not willing to give up hope, Vera looked for the courage to think of other options.

They decided to investigate a surrogate and began reviewing photos and backgrounds of several surrogates before deciding on one.

Her name was Hollie. She was in her late 20s, married and had three kids of her own. Hollie was blessed with easy pregnancies and wanted to help other couples struggling to have their own children. Both Vera and Dave thought she was terrific, with great energy and kindness. They decided to go ahead with in vitro fertilization, but Hollie did not get pregnant.

Vera and Dave were both devastated. Vera felt maybe this was a sign from God that they were not supposed to have children together. She thought about what she and Dave would do next.

Hollie wanted to try again, and this time it took! Hollie was pregnant with twins. Vera and Dave were very excited, but Vera was cautious because there were still nine months ahead.

Hollie had a very healthy pregnancy up to the sixth month, when she had to have a special procedure—one with only a 50% success rate—in order to prevent her from going into early labor. Vera was worried that once again their dream of having a child would not become a reality. She stayed focused in prayer and kept a positive attitude. Dave, Vera and Hollie made it through the next few months and were blessed with two beautiful boys—Kyle and Logan.

Vera and Dave's family would not have been complete without Hollie's dedication, love and care for the boys while she was pregnant. Even when times got difficult with medication and hospitalization, Hollie persevered, doing whatever it took to bring these boys into the world. Vera believes that God had sent them an angel to carry their children. They grew to love Hollie and her family as if they were blood-related.

Vera was 46 when her children were born and couldn't believe she was actually holding her two amazing boys. She appreciates the miracle of her children every day. She looks forward to sharing with her sons the story of how much they were wanted and how special their birth was. Vera's story is one of courage in the face of frustration and many setbacks. She constantly looked for alternative options and prayed the right opportunities would present themselves. And somehow they did … Kyle and Logan are living proof of that!

"You can't live a perfect day without doing something for someone who will never be able to repay you."

JOHN WOODEN

"*Courage is the power to let go of the familiar.*"

RAYMOND LINDQUIST

GIVING VOICE

~ by Kathleen Everett

I met Kathleen through Mary Anne Radmacher, who wrote the foreword to this book. Kathleen is a wonderful woman and author who shared this beautiful story with me about her canary giving her a voice. Here is her story ...

A gift from my children for a long-ago Mother's Day, when we met he was young and very much alive ... brilliant orange with yellow tail feathers. For his abode, the children chose a turquoise and white cage reminiscent of the Taj Mahal.

They selected him for his beauty and because they were told he would sing. I was thrilled. We settled him into his palace, hung the bells and toys, and began the great family tradition known as "Naming the Pet." Any parent can tell you this is far more complicated than "Naming The Child" because during the latter process the child doesn't get to vote. Since consensus could not be reached, the talks were tabled pending a sign from the universe. As the days went on, the new little one never uttered a sound. I read everything I could about canaries and grappled with the philosophical dilemma of keeping a bird in a cage . . . wondering whether his silence was a form of protest. I thought perhaps he was lonely. Researching the social requirements of a canary, I learned that introducing a companion could incite an ugly battle to the death. He was eating, drinking and playing with the toys, so I figured maybe a little speech therapy was in order.

Our local library had very few choices in the "books on tape for birds" section. I ended up borrowing *An Audio Guide to Duck Calls* and *North American Bird Songs*. I hoped these wouldn't turn out to be too confusing for a canary. For all I knew I'd be playing a tape that said "have a nice day and watch out for cats" in 52 dialects. But it was all our library had to offer.

So every day we listened to the tapes, followed by free time when I turned on the radio or CDs, trying all kinds of music. He listened without comment to Ella Fitzgerald, Led Zeppelin, Chopin and The Dixie Chicks. I even whistled and sang for him to model the open-your-mouth-and-have-sound-emerge concept, in case he had forgotten about that option. We kept up this routine for three weeks. I called the library and was told I could renew the tapes, as there was not a waiting list for them.

I also called the store where he had been purchased in case there was something else I should be doing. The staff told me to be sure he was not near a draft and he had a covered place to retreat to as needed.

"Oh" they said, "and sometimes a *he* turns out to be a *she*, and therefore won't ever sing." So if I wasn't happy, I could return the bird. But that was not an option for me. I'd invested too much love to turn back, and it felt very unethical to fault a creature for not being born male. So I continued our daily tutoring sessions, and he or she kept me company as I worked, though our conversations remained one-sided.

Then one afternoon, while Ronan Tynan, one of the Three Irish Tenors, was singing "My Wild Irish Rose," a very loud high-pitched song wailed along with him. I was ecstatic. The little canary continued singing through the end of that tune and into the next. I put the CD on "continual repeat" and he sang all afternoon. Since Ronan Tynan could be the poster child for triumph over adversity, I was certain this was the sign we'd been waiting for.

When the children came home from school, the Irish tenor and the Avian soprano were still performing their duet. Our canary was immediately and unanimously named Ronan. To congratulate our little champion and spur him on to further feats of greatness, I cut out a picture of Mr. Tynan from the Irish Tenors pinup calendar Aunt Peg had given me the year before and I hung it inside the cage near one of his perches. When I came downstairs the next morning I was horrified to see that Ronan Jr. had

ruthlessly pecked Big Ronan's eyes out. I hadn't realized that his territorial instincts would transcend species and dimension.

Undeterred, I cut out new pictures of the "Great Role Model," this time taping them to the outside of the cage. This gave him an unfortunate incarcerated look, but one that was preferable to the gruesome images of my hero with his eyes poked out. Ronan, the canary, sang his way through the years that followed, while the children grew up and the world changed around him.

He patiently listened as I realized that big changes needed to be made in my own world. I practiced speaking clearly and without digression while Ronan listened. He quietly sat on his perch while I explained that while I understood this would be very difficult, and it was not a decision I had come to lightly, there was no other option. Some days I wavered in my courage and wondered aloud if in fact I should just quietly surrender and stay put. So many lives are impacted when a family comes apart. I told him that I had run out of hope, and that this was not easy for me, either. If Ronan grew weary of my angst-ridden monologues, he never showed it. By listening and commenting with only an occasional chirp, my little feathered Buddha helped me to articulate the things that really mattered, and eliminate those that might be unnecessary or unkind.

Over time this certainty worked its way down to my feet and helped me stand unwavering in the decision to end my 20-year marriage. I reassured Ronan we were in this together and that *no matter what*, he would get his Fruity Treats. He continued to fill our home, before and after the big move, with his beautiful songs.

A few years later, on a gray morning in November, I came downstairs to find that my sweet Ronan had died. He hadn't shown any signs of illness, though he had been less vocal in recent months. We had been together for 10 years, a nice long life by canary standards.

I remain grateful to my sweet Ronan.

I thought he needed me to help him find his voice; turns out it was the other way around.

*"When you come to the end of your rope,
tie a knot and hang on."*

FRANKLIN D. ROOSEVELT

Soulful
CONNECTIONS

Parents are not supposed to bury their children. It takes a special brand of courage to make it through the day after such a horrific event. One such mom, Sally, shared some amazing stories of how she learned to cope … and the special connection she shared with her son.

Sally's son, Jake, was driving with a friend six months before his senior graduation. An excellent student and artist, Jake was also a very good driver. But an older intoxicated man ran into Jake's car going 60 mph and Jake had to be airlifted from the accident.

Jake had several surgeries to try to repair the damage, but he was brain dead and on life support. Many of his friends came to the hospital with art, poems, stories and prayers to support Jake, but after a few days he passed away.

Several months after his accident, Sally was home alone and she had the most unusual tingling sensation in her toes and legs. She suddenly had this thought to open a store to help others who were grieving—an angel store.

Sally called her boyfriend to share this story and he asked her where the thought had come from. Suddenly she heard a snap and a noise at the end of the hallway. It sounded like loud static. The noise was coming from Jake's room and when she opened the door, his clock radio alarm was going off. It hadn't been on since the morning he got up for school on the day of his accident.

That was enough of a sign for her. Sally opened the angel store only three months after the accident, working at it for seven months. While the store wasn't profitable, it had served its purpose, helping her with her grief and allowing her to heal, while comforting others along the way.

There were still months of crying and sadness over losing Jake, but Sally learned ways to manage her grief. Although Jake was gone, his soul and spirit were bigger than his short life here on earth.

One day, Sally was doing an older woman's hair at the salon she owned. The woman, who didn't know about her son said, "Your son is a very special boy," and told Sally that Jake left a message for her under his bed.

Sally was shocked and told the woman that her son had passed away. Still, Sally ran home that night, went to Jake's bed and looked under it. He had put art papers under his bed—drawings that Sally had never seen before and probably would have never found if this woman hadn't told her to look there.

Our connection with our loved ones exceeds time or even our physical world. Sally will always have a soulful connection with her son.

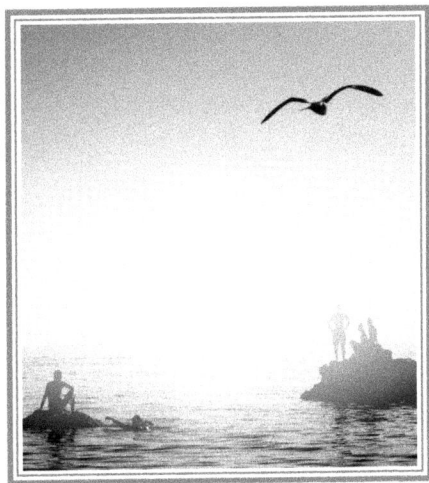

"That Love is all there is,
Is all we know of Love."

EMILY DICKINSON

"*By failing to prepare, you are preparing to fail.*"

BENJAMIN FRANKLIN

EYES WIDE OPEN

Sometimes we can get blindsided by the events that happen in our lives. Certified Financial Planner Rebecca Kennell shares the story of two of her clients, Pam and Tom, whose lack of planning could have been averted with the courage to take responsibility for the future.

Both in their fifties, Pam and Tom had not really done any long-term financial planning. Theirs was a second marriage, and Tom knew he should have a will or trust, but somehow he just didn't get around to it. Soon after Tom and Pam's meeting with Rebecca, Tom had a bicycle accident. The resulting x-rays revealed lung cancer and he passed away three months later, with the will kit still in the closet.

Without a will, a bitter probate battle developed. Tom and Pam had only been married a year and a half and the life insurance policy that Tom held listed his daughter, rather than Pam, as beneficiary. The result? Probate lasted two years, causing Pam a great deal of stress and costing her $30,000 in court costs. Suffering from a lack of sleep and distraught by the double impact of the death of her spouse and fighting with his daughter, Pam finally turned to anti-depressants to help balance herself emotionally. She developed physical effects, ranging from skin rashes to stomach problems—she was a mess, both physically and emotionally. Tom's death caused her deep heartache and presented problems she was never prepared to handle.

Pam was not very sophisticated financially when she married Tom, and he was just beginning to teach her about his assets when he passed away. She didn't bring a lot of assets or income to the marriage and mistakenly felt she didn't have the "right" to discuss these topics then. This is an error Rebecca sees many times in counseling clients. "If you are entering into a marriage partnership, you not only have a 'right' to discuss all of these topics, you should discuss them to avoid any future miscommunication," Rebecca advises.

Although Pam felt overwhelmed by this extremely stressful situation, she swallowed her pride and became wiser financially and stronger physically. She began to take charge of her own financial future—learning what to fight for in probate and what to let go of. Even more importantly, with Rebecca's help, she became financially savvy ... understanding her assets and setting up her own trust.

"A lot of people are in denial about end-of-life planning," says Rebecca. "But that really turns out to be a selfish decision, one that leaves everyone around you having to make very hard choices. Sometimes it starts disagreements that can last for a generation."

Not only did Pam have to make end-of-life decisions for Tom, she had to deal with his daughter and an ex-wife who was still very angry at Tom for their divorce two years earlier. The best gift you can give your loved ones is putting your plan in place so there's no guesswork or disagreement in an emotionally stressful time.

Rebecca suggests taking small steps to protect your future. "It's important to be prepared," says Rebecca. "It can start with something as small as getting organized—having file folders and putting beneficiary information in a file for both spouses to share. Sometimes it just takes one spouse stating the obvious to get the conversation started, 'If something happens, I'll need to take over for the two of us. If I can't find things, they might be lost forever.'"

Smart planning doesn't only relate to end-of-life decisions. "While no one goes into marriage thinking about divorce, it's something that affects a lot of couples in this country," says Rebecca. "Women lose a lot of their inheritance through death or divorce when documents aren't updated." As one of our clients said, "I don't want to be sad and broke."

Death and divorce are highly emotional times. It takes courage to take the long view and protect yourself for the future before these events happen. Death is inevitable and divorce affects millions every year. As Rebecca says, "You can't stick your head in the sand and think that it won't happen to me."

"*Courage is the most important of all the virtues, because without courage you can't practice any other virtue consistently. You can practice any virtue erratically, but nothing consistently without courage.*"

MAYA ANGELOU

"Yesterday I dared to struggle. Today I dare to win."

BERNADETTE DEVLIN

Just the
TWO OF US

~ By BJ Gallagher

I'll never forget that first night in our new apartment. I had spent the previous week getting the place ready for us to move in as I prepared for the next chapter in my life: a single mom going back to college with my four-year-old son, Michael, in tow.

We had lived with my parents in Dover, Delaware, for a year after my marriage broke up. They were so patient and generous as they gave me space and time to figure out what I was going to do with the rest of my life. I was just 23 years old—disappointed in love and confused about my future. I finally decided I needed to go to college and get an education.

I had very little money to start my new life—$100 a month child support and $100 a month from my parents. I rented a basement apartment in Newark, where the University of

*"Just remember,
you can do anything you
set your mind to, but it takes
action, perseverance, and
facing your fears."*

GILLIAN ANDERSON

Delaware was located, a hundred miles north of Dover. I furnished it with a $10 army cot for Michael, a $40 used bed for myself, a $10 table on which to study, and two empty beer kegs with pillows on top for stools. My coffee table was two cinderblock bricks with a board across the top. There was no sofa, just a small Greek flokati rug to sit on the floor. A bookcase held my radio/receiver, turntable and a pair of small stereo speakers. The apartment looked like a typical college student apartment, except that in our case, the student was a young single mother with a toddler.

Michael and I spent our first day unpacking and putting our clothes and personal things away in the closets and cabinets. His toys filled a plastic laundry basket. We went to the market to stock up on food and got the kitchen all ready to use. It had been a busy day.

Bedtime came and after his bath, I knelt to tuck Michael into his army cot. Tears welled up in his eyes as I leaned over to kiss him goodnight. "I'm scared," he started to cry. "I want to go back to Grandma's house."

I wrapped my arms around him. "I know, sweetheart. I want to go back to Grandma's house too," I said as I started to cry, too. "But we can't—we have to stay here and start our new life. From now on it's just you and me."

We clung to each other and sobbed. We felt like a couple of orphans, suddenly finding ourselves alone that night, knowing we had to make our own way in the world.

There were no reassuring bedtime stories or fairy tales to make us feel better. We just hugged each other. Michael finally fell asleep in my arms and I went off to sleep in my own room.

That was many years ago and needless to say, we survived that night. We rose to the challenges of the following days, weeks, months and years. It wasn't easy for either of us. I often say that Michael and I took turns raising each other.

And we still like to go to Grandma's house—but we're not afraid to sleep in our own beds, in our own homes, anymore.

"*Courage is not the towering oak that sees storms come and go, it is the fragile blossom that opens in the snow.*"

ALICE MACKENZIE SWAIM

Co-Dependent
NO MORE

When Steve and Jo met, it was a whirlwind romance. Steve professed his love for Jo daily and took her to the best restaurants and on wonderful vacations. He gave her beautiful gifts and told her he was going to marry her, that he knew right from the moment he met her. Jo felt so lucky to be with Steve—he was funny, charming, intelligent and creative. He had a plan for a beautiful life for both of them and she was swept away.

A talented musician and artist, Steve had charisma. He was the life of the party, but she noticed that he would get really drunk when they went to parties. He was never mean or angry, just funny and sarcastic.

All of that changed right after their wedding. Steve would get drunk and have horrible nights screaming and verbally abusing Jo. The next day he would cry and apologize, promising he would never drink that much again.

Although Jo was hurt by all the terrible things Steve said, she knew it was the alcohol talking. This was her wonderful husband, so she committed to helping him get better. Jo demanded that Steve seek counseling. They both went for several months. Steve would make promises at first, but then he started coming to their sessions drunk. He attended more group therapy sessions as a result of his poor behavior, but Jo wondered if any of it was really helping. Steve would have a "breakthrough" of enlightenment after a session, but a few days later he would be back to his same old ways.

What was Jo going to do? The counselors told her to read books on co-dependency and explained that she was part of the problem, not the solution. But how could she give up on her husband and her marriage?

Jo told me she never felt as lonely as she did in her own marriage. She was really good at keeping up the façade, but people close to her knew she had changed and was unhappy.

Finally, one night she drove home to find her husband drunk again, using foul language. The caged animal came out of her, and she lunged across the table at him, started strangling him and couldn't stop. Luckily, she finally took charge of her emotions. She let go and ran out the door to her car, knowing at that moment that her marriage was over. She had turned into a person she despised. She had no control over her emotions and could have easily hurt her husband in that moment. When did this all happen? Jo was a sweet, smart, pretty girl with an aspiring career, but everything changed after her marriage.

The night she attempted to strangle Steve changed everything for Jo. She realized that she couldn't control her own anger and her addiction to this horrible relationship. She had to leave and make changes in her life.

Jo consulted a lawyer and began to pull her savings together to start her life over. The fear of her own anger toward Steve kept her away from him. She had to find the strength and courage to believe there was a better life for her.

Steve was furious and continued trying to manipulate Jo, leaving her threatening messages all night long. He broke her personal items in the house and changed all the locks and bank accounts, cutting her off financially and personally. Jo was scared and wondered how she was ever going to get out of this horrible mess.

The one saving grace was Jo's counselor. He was patient with her, giving her the tools to handle herself emotionally. Steve followed the same script many nights—an angry alcoholic acting out. Jo's best defense was to be prepared with a great offense, trying her best not to take things personally. The horrible things Steve said about her would never leave her mind, but she knew it was the alcohol talking. She continued to move forward, taking small steps each day.

She learned to set boundaries and not let him enrage her. Jo met with other women in the same situation and started to understand that she was not alone in her embarrassment and fears. She leaned on her family and friends for support, asking them to help her maintain her boundaries with Steve. Jo also kept a journal, writing down her feelings and thoughts, knowing she could look back on them if she started to become weak again.

After a three-year battle, Jo got a divorce. She has moved on with her life and is happier and healthier.

Jo is now dedicated to helping other women get out of abusive alcoholic relationships. She volunteers at a women's center and teaches self esteem classes. Jo has found her voice and independence again and never wants to lose it to another destructive relationship. Through her volunteer work, she hopes to help other women muster the courage to find their voices too.

"Success is not final, failure is not fatal:
it is the courage to continue that counts."

WINSTON CHURCHILL

"*Pain nourishes courage.*
You can't be brave if you've only had
wonderful things happen to you."

MARY TYLER MOORE

MY STORY
"I asked not why ...
but what for."

It was November 2008, when I was diagnosed with breast cancer. I was only 38 years old and it came as a complete shock. When I first heard the news from my doctor, I fell to my knees and started crying.

Could this really be true? Perhaps the lab results were a false positive? I really didn't know anything about cancer and specifically breast cancer. I knew I needed to gather more facts and get a second opinion, so I put together a list of all the expert physicians I knew to get recommendations for breast cancer specialists. I searched the Internet for everything I could find on breast cancer.

Armed with a notebook with all of my questions, I made an appointment with my doctor to discuss my options. Unfortunately my tumor had tested positive for invasive cancer. My doctor could not confirm if the cancer had spread elsewhere in my body until they removed some of my lymph nodes in surgery.

I really couldn't believe what I was hearing. I didn't feel sick—other than the instant pain in my stomach from the news of testing positive for cancer. I was healthy and very active—someone who loved to hike, bike, do yoga and Pilates. I ate healthy foods the majority of the time and was not overweight. While I had my fair share of stress in my life, overall I was a healthy person. Why was this happening to me?

There was cancer on both sides of my family, but only later in years; when my grandfather and aunt were in their 60s and my grandmother was in her 50s. Cancer had never crossed my mind as something I would have to worry about in my 30s. I had not even lived my life yet.

The "C" word has such a negative stigma—one that connotes confusion and fear—and immediately brings to mind anxiety and sadness. People around you are not prepared to handle this kind of news. I could barely tell people that I was diagnosed. And when I did, many of my friends would break down in tears. There were so many unanswered questions. How was I going to face this battle? How was I going to run my business and my life? I still wanted to have children, and I started to regret waiting to have a family.

I gathered all the information I had researched and then meditated by myself or with my friend, Trina, on what decision would be best for me. I really believe God was listening. There are no perfect answers for dealing with cancer; you have to do what feels comfortable and right to you. I finally decided I was going to have a lumpectomy and removal of my lymph nodes. Then we would decide what to do next. One decision at a time—it was extremely overwhelming.

Since I knew that I may not have a chance to get pregnant if I had to go through chemotherapy, I went to a fertility doctor and told him that I wanted to freeze my eggs. We didn't have much time—it was only one month before my surgery. There was some risk, but my doctors agreed that if I harvested the eggs quickly before surgery, the cancer cells would not spread since my cancer tested positive to estrogen and progesterone. While I was fully aware of the consequences, it was a risk I was willing to take. Thankfully the procedure was successful.

I had my lumpectomy right before Christmas. It took an hour longer than expected and my surgeon was careful and meticulous not to remove too much tissue. Unfortunately, after my lab results came back, the doctor informed me that they had not cleared the margins enough and needed to do another surgery. I couldn't believe my ears!

Luckily, my five lymph nodes came back negative for cancer and my MRI did not show that it had spread to any other areas of my body. I opted to have another lumpectomy and this time, they got all the cancer. I then started eight weeks of radiation treatments.

Those eight weeks were very painful and tiring, both mentally and physically. Lying on a hard surface in a cold room, I watched the huge "bank-vault" silver door slowly close. You are all alone in this room and remain separated from others because of the harmful radiation. You can't help but think, "Is this really going to make me healthy?" It seemed more like a daily torture chamber at the time, and it was exhausting. But, somehow with the help of my caring doctors and my friends, I made it through and luckily didn't have to go through chemotherapy.

A few weeks later, my mammogram was negative for breast cancer and I was on my way to recovery.

I have met so many wonderful cancer survivors, with whom I share a bond and level of empathy that I can't explain. While I certainly wouldn't have chosen it, cancer has brought me many new inspirational friends who have all taught me different lessons. One of the most important is to not become a victim to this disease ... to persevere and move forward positively with my life. Each day is precious and I am reminded to be present with my family and friends, appreciating all the goodness that surrounds me.

I was recently very moved by a quote from Andrea Ivory, a breast cancer survivor and CNN 2009 Hero, who said, "I asked not why, but what for." That is a terrific philosophy to follow: to wonder what I am supposed to do with this knowledge and experience and how I can positively impact others. Andrea has already done something with her experience. She has started a mobile mammography service in Florida offering free screenings for women.

I have had many challenges in my life so far, but I am a stronger person for having them. With new opportunities and friendships, I have a clearer vision of what is truly important in my life and future. God has given me a new lease and I am going to do some great things with this one!

Without the challenges I've faced, I believe I would have never had this opportunity to write this book. When I met Mac Anderson, I was going through my battle with breast cancer and I shared my story with him one night, discovering he was a cancer survivor himself. He immediately became my motivator and mentor. Since Mac happens to be in the business of motivating others to do their very best, I think God knew I needed some serious motivation and sent me one of His "star" team members.

Mac sent me inspirational cards and books before and after my surgery and during my weeks of radiation, with sincere words of encouragement. He is definitely an example of someone who practices what he preaches. I turned to several of his books when I felt like I couldn't go any further and they reminded me to keep working and do a little better each day. I hope that by sharing my stories of other women with great courage, you will find inspiration too. Don't look for the roar ... look for the "quiet voice" of courage to get you through tomorrow.

"*Believe in yourself!*
Have faith in your abilities!
Without a humble but reasonable confidence
in your own powers you cannot
be successful or happy."

NORMAN VINCENT PEALE

ABOUT MARY ANNE RADMACHER
(Author of the foreword and the poem)

Mary Anne Radmacher loves to craft words and understand, in the silences between them, the way to create meaning in art and in life. Her words and works have been available commercially for decades in the form of books, greeting cards, posters and assorted gift products. She is included in the Oxford Dictionary of American Quotations. Her words and stories of inspiration taken from her works circle the globe.

Mary Anne enjoys offering inspiration through speaking and teaching. She leads guided writing processes online and in person that help others pursue their own writing practice. Mary Anne has published several books with Conari Press, among them: *Courage Doesn't Always Roar, May Your Walls Know Joy,* and *Promises to Myself,* all available at **www.redwheelweiser.com** or wherever books are sold.

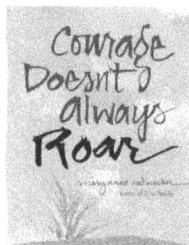

Mary Anne is honored by the variety of places in which her words and works appear. Still, she insists, the greatest honor is when a child says she is a "fun" person and assesses that she knows how to play and dance well.

About Author Bobi Seredich

Bobi Seredich enjoys connecting others and building relationships. She is the President and founder of Equanimity, Inc. (EQspeakers), a speakers bureau and training company. She is also the co-founder of the Southwest Institute for Emotional Intelligence. She has over 18 years of experience in event planning, corporate training and the speaking industry. The speakers that her company represents are incredibly talented thought leaders positively changing our world. Bobi is passionate about teaching and inspiring others. She has worked in the U.S. and all over the world with Fortune 500 clients as well as smaller companies wanting to create high performing leaders and teams.

Bobi lives in Phoenix, Arizona where she has been involved in the community with many charity groups including Multi-Cultural Arts Foundation, Tom Crawford Leadership Children's Foundation, Susan G. Komen Foundation, Sister to Sister Heart Awareness Foundation, and currently teaches classes for the Fresh Start Women's Foundation. She enjoys hiking, biking, yoga and Pilates. She loves to travel and has been to twenty-six countries. One of her favorite morning rituals is walking her two dogs, Boofalena and Louis.

Bobi can be reached at bobi@EQspeakers.com.

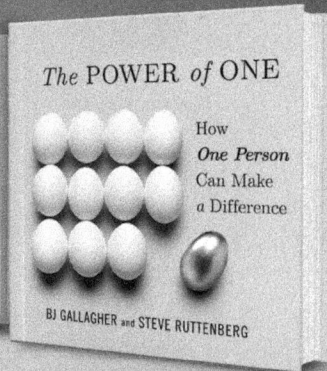